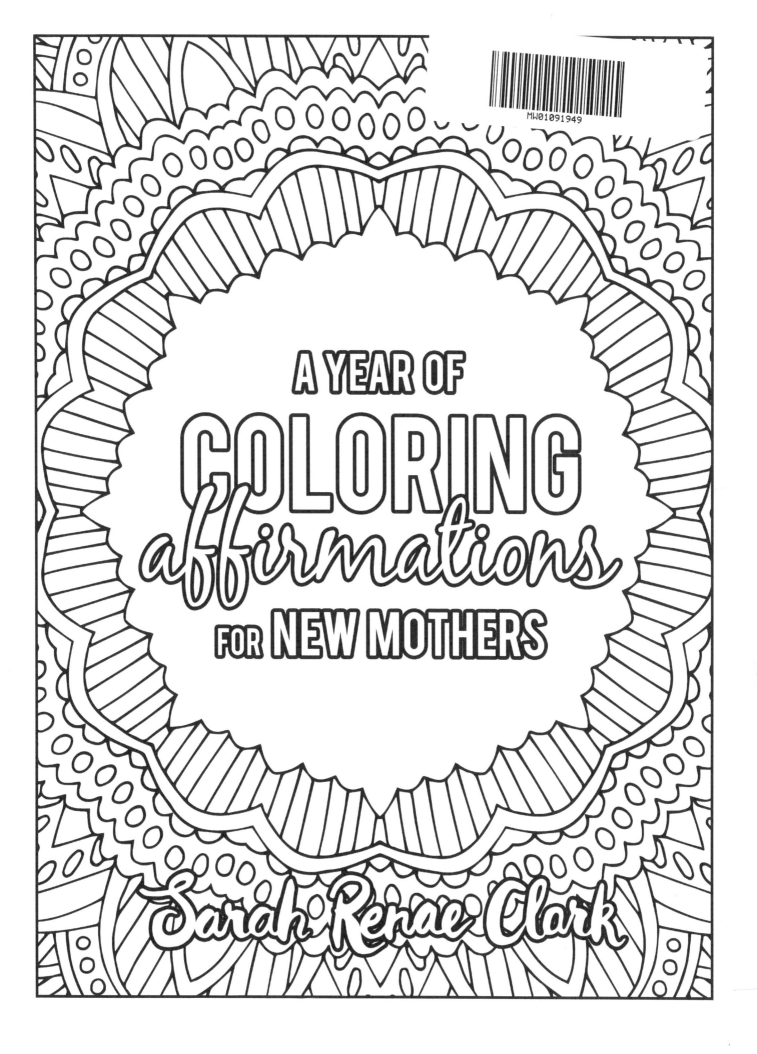

A YEAR OF
COLORING
affirmations
FOR NEW MOTHERS

Sarah Renae Clark

I want to dedicate this book to my amazing husband, Shane.

In my journey as a new mother and as an artist, you have
supported me through every high and low. I love you and I couldn't
have done this without you.

Cover colored by Debbie Shepard

Back cover images colored by:
Linda Franklin, Amber Brooks, Debbie Shepard, Emma Turnbull and Michelle H-H

www.SarahRenaeClark.com
Facebook.com/sarahrenaeclark
Instagram.com/sarahrenaeclark

FROM ONE MOTHER TO ANOTHER...

This book includes 52 pages of positive affirmations to give new mothers the encouragement, confidence, inner strength and coping abilities they need to get through the unexpected ups and downs of the early years of motherhood.

I have created the pages of this book during my own challenging days in my first year as a new mother.

I had a long and traumatic labor that resulted in our little boy being in the special care nursery for a few days after the birth. I struggled with anxiety and post-traumatic stress for about 24 hours after the delivery, when I kept reliving the delivery and thinking I was still in labor. I didn't have my little baby in my arms to remind me that it was over, and we went home without him, which was one of the hardest things that I never expected we would have to do. After a few days, we were able to finally take him home and begin our journey into the new world of parenthood.

It took me a few months to realize that I wasn't coping like I should. Our little baby was doing so well – other than some reflux issues, he was a very healthy little boy, he slept really well, and he got into a great routine. But there were days that I just wanted to collapse in a corner and cry. I felt guilty that I wasn't able to cope, since he was such a "good baby". I had a very supportive network of family and friends, but family weren't close enough to stop by regularly and I didn't want to ask the same friends for help again and again.

Motherhood is something that nobody can really prepare for. You can read every book, follow every routine, do everything right, have the "perfect" baby, and still not cope. Sometimes it's hormones, sometimes it's post natal depression, and sometimes it's just a bad day.

In those moments, it's hard to ask for help, but sometimes all it takes is an encouraging word or a boost of confidence to get through. One positive thought can change your entire day.

The word "affirmation" comes from the Latin affirmare, originally meaning "to make steady, strengthen." When we affirm and meditate on positive thoughts, we empower ourselves to get through and actually see a change in our thinking, feelings, emotions and mental health.

Affirmations can sometimes feel forced and it can be hard to embrace them. We are encouraged by experts to repeat our affirmations out loud, multiple times a day. Coloring affirmations combine the therapeutic art of coloring with the power of positive thinking and visualization. Through the meditation and mindful focus of coloring, you are absorbing the positive message on each page without having to force yourself to repeat it. You are expanding the concept of positive affirmations to appeal to more of your senses – rather than just speaking and hearing, you can now touch and visualize as well. By working on the same page for multiple days, you are establishing positive thoughts in your long term memory and changing your entire way of thinking.

Designing these pages has been therapeutic to me through my hard days as a new mother, and I hope that coloring them will help you too.

Not loving every moment of MOTHERHOOD doesn't mean I don't love being a MOTHER

My child loves me
My child trusts me

IF I DO NOTHING TODAY OTHER THAN HUG MY BABY THEN I'VE DONE ENOUGH

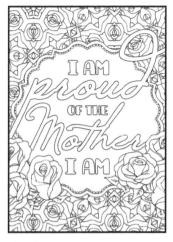

I AM proud OF THE Mother I AM

I am beautiful

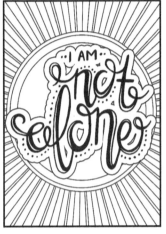

I AM not alone

I can face any problem that comes my way

If I'm out of my pajamas by noon it's a great day

THIS TOO SHALL PASS

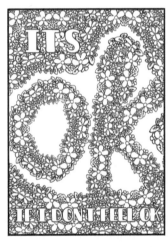

IT'S OK IF I DON'T FEEL OK

Motherhood is the HARDEST job in the WORLD AND I'M DOING GREAT

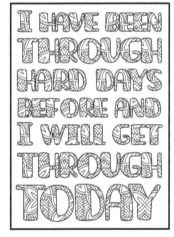

I HAVE BEEN THROUGH HARD DAYS BEFORE AND I WILL GET THROUGH TODAY

TODAY I WILL SEE THE BEST IN MY CHILD AND THE BEST IN MYSELF

I AM FULL OF ENERGY

I am the BEST PERSON To raise my CHILD

I know that EVERYTHING is going to be OK!

SHARE YOUR JOURNEY

Share your colored pages with me
#coloringaffirmations

www.sarahrenaeclark.com

facebook.com/sarahrenaeclark
instagram.com/sarahrenaeclark

I HAVE BEEN THROUGH HARD DAYS BEFORE AND I WILL GET THROUGH TODAY

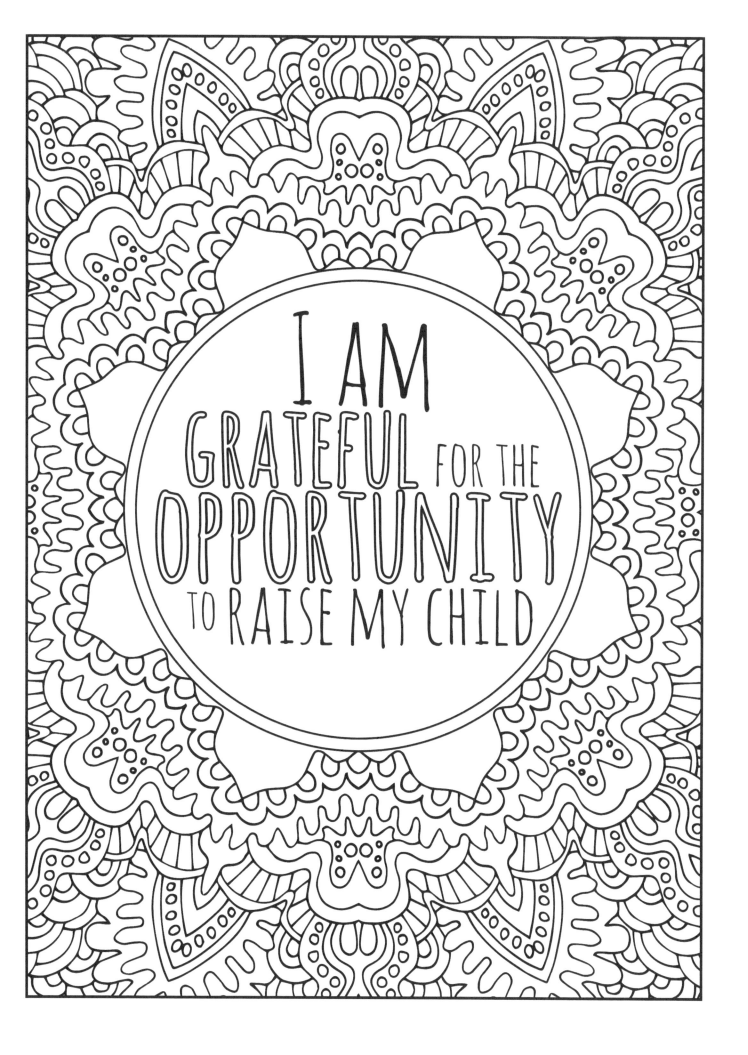

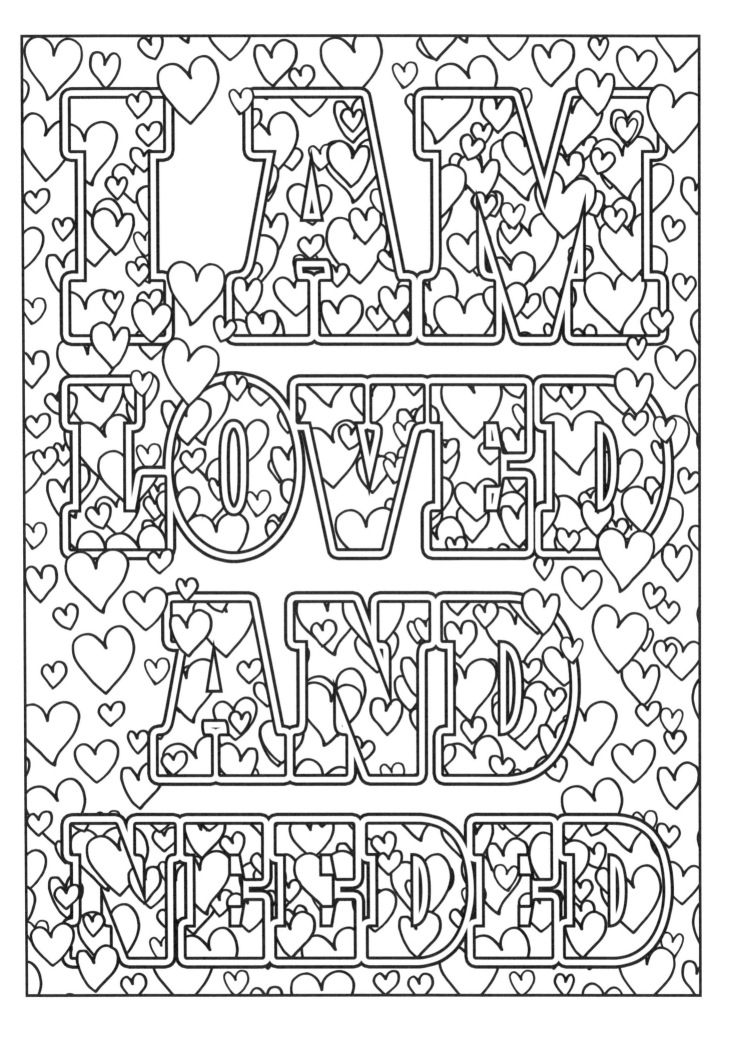

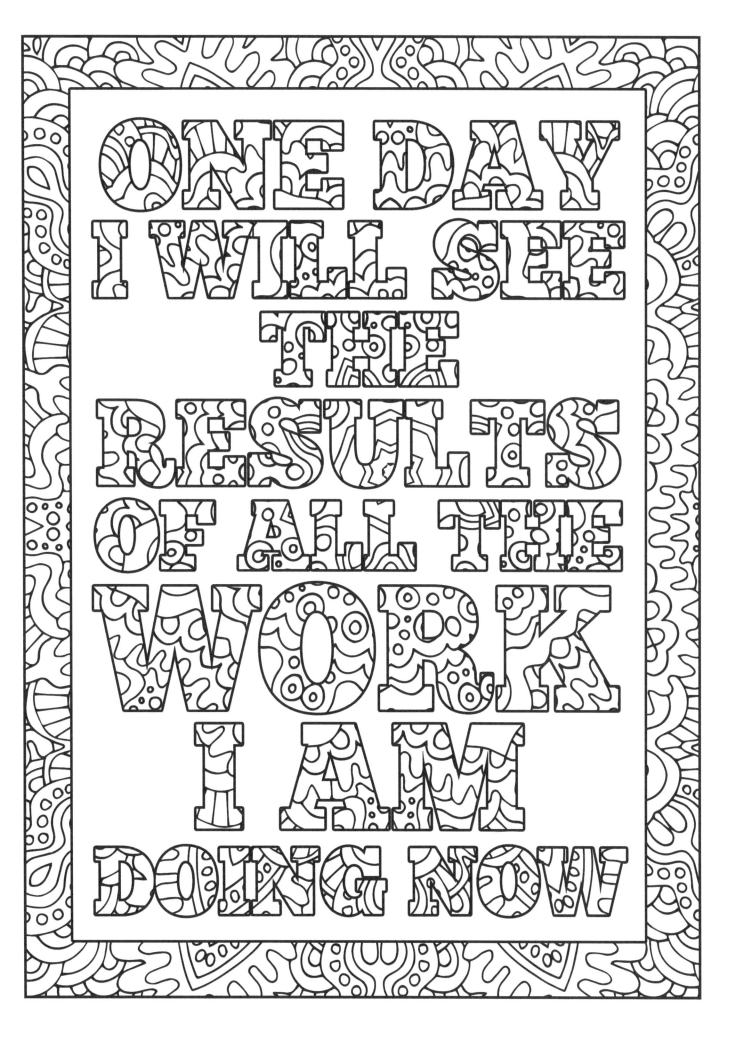

EVERY LITTLE THING I DO FOR MY CHILD IS BUILDING TOWARDS A WONDERFUL FUTURE FOR THEM

USE THIS COLOR WHEEL TO COMPARE COLORS AND SHADES!

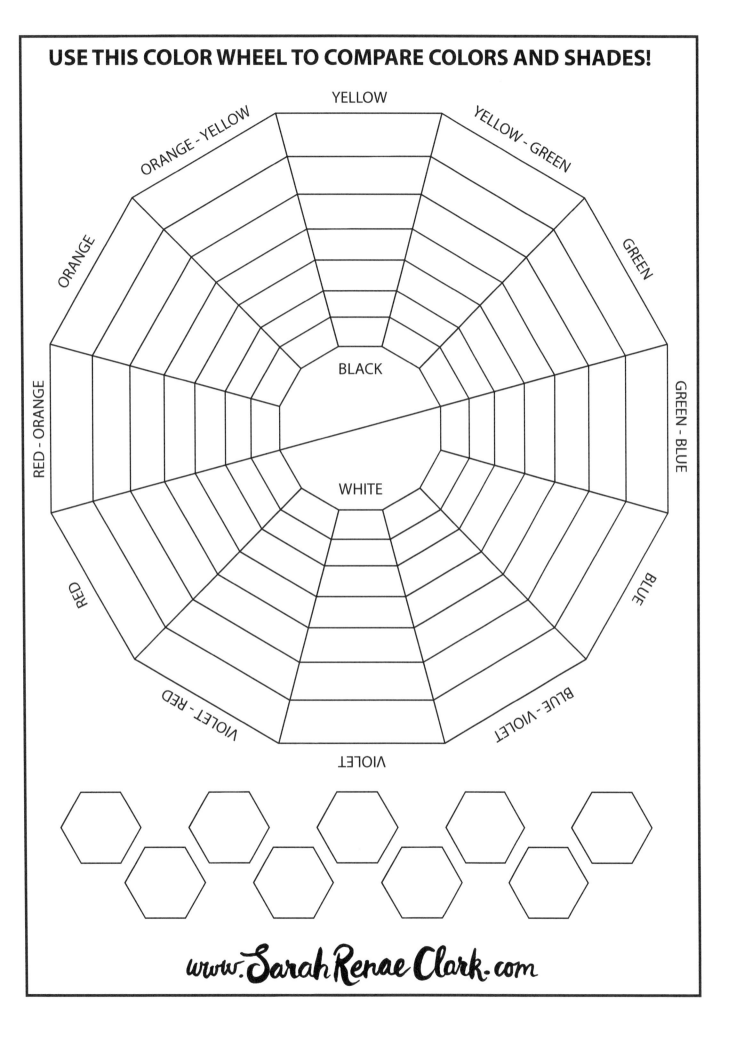

THANK YOU!

I hope you've enjoyed coloring!

Don't forget to share your colored pages with me
and join other mothers on their journey!
#coloringaffirmations

facebook.com/sarahrenaeclark
instagram.com/sarahrenaeclark

I invite you to come and visit my website for more
coloring books, free coloring pages and
personalized pages you can print from home!

www.SarahRenaeClark.com

Made in United States
Troutdale, OR
11/14/2024

24799149R00064